First Kiss

How To Create An Ideal Opportunity For Intimate Physical Contact And Successfully Carry Out Impeccable Kissing Technique

Rick anBree

Then nothing happened.

Emily didn't even reply. She didn't take her eyes off the throng behind her. On her right, a man appeared out of nowhere. When he approached Emily, he already had a glass in his hand.

"Hey, lovely! A little too loudly, he remarked, "Let me buy you a drink." You could easily see that guy was inebriated.

Sherry, who was now standing right behind Emily, remarked, "She already has one." Emily was not even aware that Sherry had left her side.

"Oh, my poor, tiny mother. I didn't realise she was yours," he said with a slur.

With a voice as steely as steel, Sherry stated, "You should move away now."

"Okay, okay," the guy said with his hands lifted in the air. He turned and disappeared into the mob.

Emily lifted her eyebrows and turned to face Sherry while using the mirror.
"I apologize for that," Sherry murmured, taking the seat beside Emily. "Some people become disrespectful idiots because they don't know when to stop."
Emily nodded and grinned. "Very true."
Okay, Emily. "What do you do?" she inquired, immediately resuming their conversation.
Emily shook her head and laughed. "I work as a Julliard teacher. I am an advanced violin instructor. How about you?

When Emily questioned Sherry about herself, her smile got bigger. She started to feel a little more at peace as the anxious flutter in her stomach subsided. She was a little nervous when she first sat down at the bar and approached her. She hadn't gone out to socialize in a while, and she felt fortunate to have met a woman of that caliber on her first night out. This indicates that it was intended to be.
"I work as an airport Customs Agent Officer. I manage all incoming data and keep an eye on the scans conducted on any targets identified as potential threats.
With genuine attention, Emily exclaimed, "Wow, that's interesting." "Is it hazardous?"
Seeing that she had impressed her, Sherry grinned broadly. It's awesome. Every now and again,

things get a little crazy, but I manage.

Sherry felt the need to go a little further after taking a few swigs from her bottle. "Do you have brothers or sisters?"

Emily thought, What a weird question to put to someone you just met at the bar. She said, sipping from her straw, "I have a brother."

Sherry's smile got bigger. "I agree with that. He has returned after a period of absence. We must share that, I suppose. Emily clarified when she saw that she was perplexed. "That our brothers are the same."

Yes, that's right. That's true," Emily remarked, growing irritated with the exchange.

Emily's favorite song started playing as the loud music downstairs continued to play. She nodded her head and began to sway to the music. She got off her stool, feeling the urge to release some steam and put an end to Sherry's litany of inquiries. She departed from Sherry at the bar with a swift wink and made her way upstairs.

Emily moved to the middle of the floor and got to dancing. With each shake and dip she took on the floor, she drove the remaining stress out of her body as the two Sangrias' calming effects started to take effect. She let the beat and bass from the speakers quicken her pulse and soothe her tension while she partially closed her eyes.

She saw the same woman from the bar walking toward her as she was dancing. Sherry approached her and fell in step with her as she continued to dance. Sherry's eyes narrowed, and her focus was fixed on Emily's figure as they danced to many songs, their bodies moving against each other in a sensuous manner.

Emily saw nothing wrong with dancing with the woman. As soon as she left the lounge, she would forget it meant nothing. She was having fun when a song started playing, and memories started to come back to her. Recollections of her enjoyable time spent dancing with Daniel at a family barbecue. Her dancing steps start to falter as the reminder of her circumstances comes with those recollections.

Her mood soured immediately, and she made the decision to go. She whirled around and headed back toward the stairs. She pushed her way across the crowded dance floor while mumbling a few "excuse me"s.

Emily started for the restroom, feeling a little flushed from dancing and the unexpected surge of feelings brought on by thoughts of Daniel. She was relieved to see that there wasn't a large queue of women waiting impatiently for once. She scurried over to the sink, turned on the cold water, and sprayed her cheeks with the refreshing mist.

She let her body calm down, then lifted her head and turned off the faucet. Just as she turned to take a paper towel, someone generously poured some into her palm. After drying her face with a pat, she turned to see who she should give thanks to.

Beside her stood a female. Her right side was shaved tight, while her hair was whipped up in one of those feather cuts that hung to the left. The woman's stunning features were further accentuated by the zigzag pattern, which further improved the cut.

Remained silent while assessing one another. Emily cast a quick glance at the woman, seeing the sparkle of her jewels and the fancy clothing. She also saw that, despite not knowing her, the woman was staring at her as if she did.

Emily responded, "Thank you," as she remembered the tissue she had just thrown in the garbage.

The woman remained silent for a brief while. She bowed her head then as though she had decided on something.

"That woman you were dancing downstairs with and sharing a drink with... heed my warning and stay clear of her. Once she sets eyes on you, run the other fucking way because she will ruin your life.

Emily scowled. She was curious, so she said, "What do you mean?"

The woman added, "Consider yourself warned," and then turned to walk away.

Confused, Emily stood there trying to figure out if the woman had been her ex-girlfriend or something. In any case, it makes no difference because I have no interest in it. After giving herself a final glance in the mirror, Emily made the decision to depart.

Sherry chased after Emily, not sure what went wrong, but she became lost in the crowd. Upon returning upstairs, at last, she discovered Emily slipping on her jacket.

"Are you heading out already?"

Startled to realize that Sherry had followed her, Emily peered up at her. Heed my warning and stayed clear of her. Yes, that's right. "I have to be somewhere," she remarked while pulling up her jacket.

Sherry's expression briefly showed disappointment, but she covered it up right away. "Well, would it be possible for me to get your phone number so I can give you a call?" She spoke with a hint of desperation, which Sherry heard but ignored. She was determined to hold onto Emily since she sensed a connection with her.

Emily turned and walked for the door without even pausing in her gait. Sherry followed closely behind her.

I'm sorry, but no, Sherry. I'm not here to meet people. All I wanted to do was relax for a bit. You know, relax."

"Oh." Sherry's forlorn expression was almost hilarious. She could feel the rejection slowly building up to rage, but Emily's next words quickly calmed her down.

Emily said, "Don't worry," as she approached the door. She winked as she glanced back over her shoulder at Sherry. She grinned and remarked, "There's always tomorrow," before vanishing into the night.

Sherry went outdoors a moment later to take a deep breath of the fresh air. She was grinning again, although she had been upset. She'd just gotten Emily's go-ahead to follow her. She was happy because she had that tiny glimmer of hope. She had a deep sense of connection with Emily, and she wasn't going to allow anything to sabotage their newfound link.

"You got shut down, huh?" a shadowy voice asked. Sherry looked over and saw a man propped up against a tree. It was nearly impossible to comprehend his inebriated mumble. Nearly. "It's because you don't have all the right tools," he laughed and grabbed his pussy.

He was the man who had rudely approached them at the pub, as Sherry had recognized. She said, "Mind your business," and then she looked to see Emily go into a taxi.

The man snorted loudly and pivoted back. That's the issue with you dyke bitches, you see. You mistakenly believe that you are a guy simply because you wear and speak like a male and have chopped your hair. However, you're not. You remain a lady. And not one of them," he said, reaching for his crotch once more. "You're not going to be a man. Never. "You'll keep failing just like tonight," he added, his gaze cold and contemptuous.

Sherry looked across at him. "You think you're a man just because you have that little flaccid penis between your legs?" Shaking her head, she laughed. "You're pitiful. She responded, "You all are," coming up to him to join him in the shadows.

He unzipped his pants and said, "If you come over here I'm going to give you something to remind you that you're a woman." He reached inside and freed his shaft with his hand. He watched her get closer, and he started to stroke it.

That's accurate. He continued, "You know you want this dick," stroking the now-hardened skin.

He was having fun in front of Sherry, and she didn't even look down. She pulled the sword from its sheath with a single, fluid motion as she approached, her hand reaching up behind her back. The metal shimmered briefly as the sharp blade cut through the muscular mass of its victim.

Sherry moved forward, thrusting the blade right under the man's chin and twisting before he could let out a cry of pain. The man choked and created bubbles out of his own blood, and all that was audible was a quiet, gurgling sound. Sherry pulled out the blade and shoved him backward away from her as she felt the weight of his body start to press into her. He tripped and fell behind the tree even further. The dimly lit lane effectively concealed his body.

Sherry took out a wad of tissue from her pocket and used it to wipe away the blood that had gotten on her hand as well as the knife. She put the knife back where it belonged, stuffed the tissue back into her pocket, and gazed into the pitch-black space where his body was lying.

"I refuse to ever be treated that way by a man again. Never again," she said to herself in a whisper. Then Emily grinned as the thought of her emerged. Her smile grew as she turned to face the area where she knew the man's body was concealed by the darkness. She turned to leave and strolled back into the lounge, saying, "I guess the better man won."

First, we headed to the movie. She was so engrossed in the movie that she never saw my hints that I wanted her to rest on my shoulder like the other couples did.

I got completely humiliated in air hockey, strangely enough, when we went to the arcade after the movie.

We finished the evening with a delicious supper. As we made our way from the restaurant to my car, I gave her my first-ever handshake.

She put both of her hands in mine as I was ready to turn on the engine. My spine tingled a million times at that one action. All evening, I had been yearning to touch her. I just stared at her, not knowing how to take hold of her and give her a passionate kiss.

She said, "I had a lot of fun tonight, Logan," just before her gaze became intensely passionate and lustful.

"Natalie, I also had the finest time. I replied in a whisper, "Thank you. She had been staring at my lips, and I only noticed that when I looked into her eyes.

"Logan...," she groaned, biting her bottom lip.

Her smile, her eyes, her voice, and her beauty drew me in once more. She continued to stare at me while breathing quickly.

I drew her in closer, not resisting. As soon as our bodies collided, we gave each other a passionate kiss. My body was overcome with the same blissful feeling that I had experienced the night I first kissed her.

I let myself become more present in the moment as I felt her tongue glide across mine. I embraced her with my arms and kissed her more deeply. I planted a passionate kiss on her while she kept groaning. Everything else was irrelevant. Time seemed to be waiting for us.

Section 8: Natalie

Even after our first date a few months ago, I still couldn't quite put my connection with Logan into words. We went on several dinner dates after our first one, and we always finished with passionate make-out sessions in his car.

Although he never made a formal courtship request, I knew he was in love with me without the help of a magician. I felt attractive and special because of him. I wanted us to be formal even though he showed me the utmost respect.

"How do I appear?" I spun around in front of Arianne and asked. I had my hair pulled back into a high ponytail and wore a pink flowery dress and white stilettos.

Arianne yawned, drowsy. "You look good all the time."

My phone beeped just as I was about to give her the finger. My heart skipped a beat when I saw that Logan had texted me to let me know he was downstairs.

I bid Arianne farewell with a peck on her cheek and headed to meet Logan. I noticed him with his arms crossed and leaned against his automobile. He wore slim-fitting pants and a black T-shirt. He looked like a model for clothing.

Upon his eventual glance up, our gazes locked, resulting in a shared smile. With each step he took toward me, his smile got bigger.

"Miss Richards, please!" He caught my waist and gave me a peck on the lips as he reddened. "You are amazing! He flung his hands around my neck and murmured, "I don't want any other man to set his eyes on you." I held him the way he loved to be held without waiting for him to ask. I cupped his waist since I knew how he liked it.

"Where are these lines coming from?" I gently pinched his cheeks while giggling.

He flinched. "Aww!"

"All set for some fun?" As he kicked the car's engine, Logan asked with a mischievous look in his eye.

When we got there, the celebration was well underway. The house smelled strongly of marijuana and alcohol. Logan held onto my waist tightly.

He yelled in my ear, "Let's make our way to the back!" His lips kissed my ear, giving me chills.

Logan led the way to his teammates' locations. I was yanked away from Logan by a crazy, inebriated guy just as we were about to sit where the rest of his team was.

"Logan!" I let out.

Logan punched the man hard right away, knocking him to the ground.

Are you alright? Logan gasped. He put his hands over my face. His breathing was labored. I put my hands around him right away. We avoided the impulse to immediately pull one other's clothes off as we stared into each other's eyes.

As his hands caressed my hips, I heard an exuberant voice exclaim, "Logan!" Julius was the one.

It's crowded here, man! Tonight is going to be really bad for me! As he drew Logan away from me, Julius remarked. Julius was pulling Logan, and Logan grabbed my hand to make sure I didn't get lost in the throng.

Eventually, we arrived at the other people's seats. Logan sat next to me, clutching my hand as though I were a treasure that had been lost and found.

Julius kept refilling my drink while I listened to the guys talk about their epic road trips and hockey.

I leaned on Logan because I was getting tipsy.

"Logan..." My head landed on his chest, and I groaned. In response, he squeezed my arms and then planted a kiss on my forehead.

"You're inebriated. He said, "I have to get you out of here.

He took me in his arms and walked out just as I was ready to fight. I overheard him telling his friends he would return soon.

I put my arms around his neck, pulled him, and gave him a sensuous lip-bite as we got closer to his car.

My abrupt movement nearly caused him to stumble. Thankfully, he was large and powerful. He eased me onto the seat after opening the rear door of the vehicle.

I dragged him back in and shut the door behind him just as he was ready to close it and turn to face the driver's seat.

Alright. I am aware that the celebration was awful.

"It wasn't." I study her face closely, but she doesn't appear to be dishing me a big helping of crap.

It was, in fact, kind of. The sole positive aspect of the entire fundraising was meeting you tonight. I immediately feel tired, so I sigh and wipe my face. "Kar, I apologize for putting that on you. Knowing that it was most likely—

Her lips are on mine. Warm, sugary, and gin-flavored. Though I'm only human, I know I should take care of whatever is bothering her. I give her a hungry kiss in return. The taste of her, her tongue, her skin that promised land between her thighs—I want to drown in it all.

As soon as we have oxygen, she gasps, "Kade, I've been thinking."

"I have not." Like, this whole night, like at all. You are wearing that outfit. I'm dying because of you. I follow the long curve of her neck with my teeth, giving me goosebumps all over.

I bite further, and her soft laugh fades into a gasp. I want to kiss her stupidly until my touch and a few profanity-laced words are all she remembers.

"Kade, this is significant. Please.

Oh, sh*t. Let's get started. Using the power of orgasms, I hoped to get her nude and convince her to let me take her out again. Well, that may sound a little dishonest, but I have no problem utilizing dubious means to persuade Karisma to go out with me once more.

I bite my lip and, stop kissing her neck reluctantly, and step back enough to meet her gaze. Her eyes are fixed on the ground, but she's gnawing on her lower lip. How in the world?

Hey, what's the deal? Are you aware that you can tell me anything? Whatever the case, Kar. I'm available to you.

Her smile came on so quickly that I thought maybe I was dreaming. Our eyes meet, and she starts talking about something serious. This is the problem. My application for corporate real estate loan financing was granted preliminary approval.

The shock I feel is the same as if she had hit me in the face. It had been a long shot, to be honest, but I really wanted this for her. And whatever became of our little talk about playing tricks on one other in bed?

She starts walking on one foot alone. B*tch. I know I'm talking too slowly, and she's going to assume the worst of me if I don't straighten out right soon.

I just say, "That's amazing," and return my face to hers. This kiss was as tender and beautiful as every couple's first kiss should be, right before she nipped at my mouth out of the blue and brought us down to a blistering fever again.

I mean it. I really do. Thank you very much. She gives a smile. I can feel her smile pressing against mine, and it makes me very pleased. I could never have finished those papers without you.

Whoa, I really must be insistent. Thank you very much. I turn my back on her and smile wildly. Was this the cause of her nervousness? Sometimes she can be so damned silly. I give her a quick back-and-forth motion after picking her up. She screams at me a few times and swings her small balled-up fists.

"So, what's all the commotion about?"

Her face becomes strained. It states, 'I need a co-signer.'" I have insufficient revenue history with the company to warrant them giving me that huge bundle of cash. She attempts a clumsy throat clearing. Would you consider acting as my co-guarantor? I don't actually need your money; I just need your wealthy status.

I give her a slow headshake. "I almost suffered a heart attack from all of this chaos. I assumed you wanted to end our relationship. Are you aware of that?

She takes a deep breath and works her throat over a knot of nervousness. "I'm not ending our relationship," I assure you. The greatest boyfriend ever is you. Reed, I apologize if I gave you the creeps. A sigh escapes her. "I find it really difficult to discuss money." particularly when I know you have a lot of it and I don't.

"Observe, Kar. We don't need to ever experience awkward situations. Anything with me should not make you feel uncomfortable, but especially not something as trivial as money.

She gives me a rolling look. "See, I understand. You've always had an abundance of money, so you don't worry about money. However, that seems like a big deal to me. I've had to work extremely hard to earn every penny I've ever received. I grew up with my parents being extremely impoverished. I've fought tooth and nail for all I've had.

I give a nod. "You're heard. I am aware of how diligent you are,

Kar—likely more so than anyone else in your life. However, you will also need to hear me out. We don't have to be separated by money. I take hold of her and give her a little shake. "Unless you allow it to, it won't come between us."

After assessing me, she nods once. Okay. Let's celebrate then, shall we? She slides to her knees and puts her hand on my dick, cutting off any logical reasoning.

It takes Kar about an hour to zip my trousers up. In any case, I'm rather certain it takes that long. My cock is pounding with all the blood in my body, so it's difficult to tell.

Finally, she grasps me, skin to skin, and I groan at her contact. It really stings to be without my clothes because I've been crushing on her for so long. Her hand is too slow but far too kind.

She's going to give me the best kind of torment tonight. I grit my teeth and tilt my head back, allowing waves of feeling to sweep over me.

I anticipate a lengthy, leisurely sequence of tender kisses, given how softly she's touching me. Rather, Kar sucks me all the way down to her throat, and I can feel her suck my entire length.

I swear that for a little minute, electric shocks shoot up my back, and my spirit leaves my body. I clench my fingers around her hair and hiss her name. Her eyes flicker open to meet mine as I gaze down at the stunning image of her on her knees, deeply engrossed in me.

She groans near my manhood. There's little doubt that this won't last nearly long enough. It would never be sufficient.

Her deft fingers are cupping my tight balls before I can even catch my breath. With an animalistic roar, I burst out and poured down her mouth.

She's staring at me with a smile that's a little naughty and a little sweet when I finally get my eyes open.

I mumble roughly, still attempting to regain my breath, "best girlfriend ever." "It's your turn again now."

K.T.

The greatest boyfriend I've ever had is Seed. He never stops giving me flowers and candies; in fact, my desk is nearly entirely covered in the different and eclectic mementos he sends me. There's a persistent joke in the area about Valentine promising to personally maintain the local flower business. It is not too bad press overall for a mayor challenging Baron von Evil in a reelection.

As it happens, Reed's reputation has benefited greatly from our relationship. It seems that many in the town are quite fond of our odd, mismatched love affair. Why wouldn't they be, after all? Everybody enjoys a good Cinderella tale, and Reed is a fantastic Prince Charming.

He comes waltzing into my office with his jacket thrown over his shoulder as if I called him by thinking about him. His smile could melt panties all around the city. I can feel a smile forming on my own lips. Horrible. Now, whenever we get together, we're going to get really mushy with one another. We are so cute together that I almost hate it.

"I'm taking you to lunch, Kar. We're going to rejoice because I have some wonderful news.

Yes, but that's my line, Mister Mayor. I jiggle a bit in my chair. "This needs to be a fast lunch, you see. Everything should be fine for the loan; I have to go to my interview with the branch manager this afternoon.

"I'm overjoyed for you." Walking towards me with a gait, I get up from my chair to greet him. I can sense his satisfaction in his kiss as he smashes his smiling mouth against mine. Whether or not he was my boyfriend, I knew he would have been eager to celebrate with me, but I much preferred Reed when he was a kissing boyfriend.

We stroll hand in hand to our favorite little Chinese restaurant, Dingho, for lunch. We even enjoy meals together, but we mainly just exchange lustful glances rather than words. He even lets me have his fortune cookie and nearly all of his noodles.

As we make our way back towards Riddles, Reed's incredibly strong arm wraps itself tightly around me. "Oh, how are you doing?" I'm actually not doing a very good job of being a friend because I was preoccupied with being in girlfriend mode with him. Girlfriend. Whatever it is, I'm meant to be doing. I am to meet the senator this afternoon at his local office, per his request. Kar, I believe he is seriously thinking about withdrawing from the race. His dazzling smile brightens everything. And it fits with the carefree little grip of his hand that he offers me because even our hands are hugging.

"Well, come see me later, and we'll celebrate at the palace in our undies." I make a tiny circle as I spin. Later on, I'll even buy you a drink. You understand, with all of my cash.

"Acquire." He gives me a little wave of his finger before loping off to engage in political activities.

I look over my portfolio for the eleventh time in the meantime. For ease of reference, every document the bank requested has been arranged and categorized. I've even packed a skirt suit complete with a formal shirt. Yes, I can put on makeup when necessary. For example, when I'm attempting to persuade people to give me large sums of money that I intend to utilize to save my company.

But I'm capable of doing this. I literally have to have only one meeting to save Riddles. I'll go in there and demonstrate to the bank manager how hard I've worked for my company and how a real estate investment may succeed in the long run with the same work ethic.

By the time I pull open the heavy front door, my palms are sweating nervously from the short trip over to the bank, even in my forced-positive mood. I clumsily make my way down the hallway, stepping like a baby deer, to the lending department.

"My name is KarismaTroudeau, and my time is 2:00." I smile politely at the receptionist, and she nods and gestures to a set of chairs that look uncomfortable and overly small.

I perch like a gaunt bird and tap my heel on the ground. I really try not to get worked up, but the more nervous I become, the longer I sit here with half of my ass dangling over this ridiculous dollhouse-sized chair.

"Ms.Troudeau?" The woman has a quiet, almost soothing voice. I turn to face the small woman with an elaborate hairstyle and elegant blouse with a bow neck.

Indeed, ma'am. It's good to meet you, I say, trailing off as I wait for her to finish introducing herself.

"Please come this way." I reach out to her, but she ignores me and walks away down a hallway with thick wood paneling and traditional wainscoting. She never, ever falters even slightly on her heels, as far as I can see.

I'm not the kind of girl who likes fancy shoes, but I try my best to keep up. I have to work twice as hard to stay upright in heels since I am so ungainly. I have to have a punchline-for-allure.

After waiting for me to catch up, she reaches the end of the corridor, knocks on the heavy door ahead of her, peers inside, and lets me know that I've arrived.

"Ms.Troudeau, please come in and take a seat." I stagger towards the bulky barrister's desk that occupies almost half of the office while she holds the door wide.

The man behind the barrister's desk gives me a slow, lascivious glance from top to bottom, clearly intending something. I have the impression that he is cataloging every detail of me for future examination after using his eyes to strip me.

He should be more than capable, depending on his recall, I think.

After all, he has witnessed everything before.

"K.T.," he exclaims, getting to his feet and coming across to embrace me.

"Jeffrey," I respond. I'm still capable of doing this. It doesn't mean I can't be professional here just because the man in front of me, who is currently pressing my rigid and unpleasant body against him, caused the largest, most terrible breakup of my life.

I still have the ability to control this circumstance. To begin with, there is absolutely no chance in hell that I will give the snake another hug. I sincerely hope he never touches me. My favorite mayor is the only one I want touching me these days; he no longer has the right to do that.

I walk back from him a little and head for the chairs in front of his desk. For the briefest moment, his mouth tightens, but I am all too familiar with that movement. He is unquestionably still the guy who, with the exception of me, always gets his wish. He was furious that he could no longer dictate to me all the time.

"K.T., it's been years. How are you doing? He crosses his arms in front of him and tilts his head at the exact angle I've seen him practice several times in front of a mirror to give me that sincere look. Since it essentially sums up Jeffrey. To acquire what he wanted from you, he would put on the persona that you required him to wear. Ultimately, it became challenging to recall his true identity when he wasn't acting.

"Well, as you can see from my loan documents, I've had a lot of success with my business here in Valentine." I take a breath, but before I can finish speaking, he's already gesturing for me to stop.

"Let's not let business talk spoil this moment." My awful former partner smiles at me with teeth.

It's interesting that I'm here to discuss just that with you. My company. I inhaled deeply once again and took out my portfolio. "If you would like to review my application, please find a copy here."

He snorts and waves his hand dismissively once more. "K.T., let's take a few minutes to catch up. What, has it been five or six years now?

"Seven and fifteen." As soon as I say those words, I want to cry. I've managed to fall straight into this particular trap that this haughty man is trying to set up with me in order to get control. Unprofessional action, Kar.

"Oh, it has been that long now? Well, it feels like yesterday already. As I sit in the supplicant's chairs in front of his enormous desk, he manspreads like it's his job, crossing one leg over the other and bringing his crotch level with my face.

I want to give him a dick punch if he doesn't want to use his lean little body as a weapon against me; at least get-up and meet my gaze. Of all people, me. I pretty much created that specific game where you use your body's strength to push others to do what you desire.

However, no. I'm in his office because I need his bank's final clearance in order to obtain a large loan large enough to purchase an entire building. Even though I'm not very knowledgeable about commercial real estate loans, I have a good feeling that my funding won't be authorized if I really give Jeffrey the finger. I mean, I can still tease him a little bit, even though I can't get harsh with him, particularly if he intends to try to trick me with mental games.

I was shocked to hear myself say that. Does the subconscious mind control a lot? The humiliation I felt when he helped me correct myself was even worse than the humiliation I felt when I was unable to look at Matt.
In order to prevent me from crashing face-first onto his easel, he grabbed my elbow with one hand,

wrapped his arm around my waist, and helped me stand up. I was pressed close to his chest, and though my body wanted to melt into him, my brain wanted me to sink into the floor.

He was taller than me by at least six inches. I discovered that his groin area was pressing against my lower rib by clutching at the stick impaling my side rather than by using my sense of vision to undertake a height analysis. A rod that was discovered to be bodily linked.

A surge of nausea surged up from my stomach's lowest point. It wasn't the nausea you get, either, when you realize that you've been walking around campus all morning with your leggings tucked inside your skirt. Nope. It was a sickness I had never experienced before, the kind that appears when you get a sneak peek at the guy you've been secretly thinking about.

My thoughts raced. What made him so tough? Was that how he usually felt?

I was wondering if he had a medical issue that gave him a permanent hard-on in between attempting to stop myself from hyperventilating and trying to get away from him, which was impossible because his arm was wrapped tightly around my waist. There was no other explanation for his excessive self-importance.

"Are you alright?" he inquired, holding onto his grip.

I made an attempt to talk. My mouth felt greasy, and when I said, "Yeah, I'm good," it sounded more like "Ahh-um-gah."

"Abbie, what is the issue?" He sounded really worried.

Apparently, my hand felt it was acceptable to inform him of the issue because my brain was deficient in oxygen. I drummed my fingertips against the bone that remained compressed in my ribcage.

"Jesus, oh!" Matt let go of me and fell from grace faster than an Instagram influencer who gets busted for content piracy. He collided with his easel, and both of them fell into a cacophonous heap.

The only sensible thing I could think of to do at that point was to laugh. I was forced to sit on the floor by my own laughter. I started crying with laughter. My laughing tears quickly transformed into a sob or two of grief—curse my frame of thinking.

Matt halted his laughter as well. "Hey," he walked menacingly and put his palm on my knee, asking, "What's wrong?"

I gave a headshake. Held her breath after taking a huge breath.

Reaching up off the floor, he held the headset in between the two of us. "Did we damage it? Will you end up in trouble?

I gave a headshake. Breathed out slowly.Not at all. Not in my opinion. Why are there so many tears?

I apologize. Simply a misplaced recollection

Matt gently and soothingly massaged my calf. "Had a horrible experience involving an easel?" I could tell he was trying to lighten the situation by smiling.

I grinned back and gave a sincere response. "A terrible erection experience."

He winced as his hand shot from my leg to his groin. "Abbie, I'm so very sorry about what happened to you. Furthermore, I apologize for making you feel uneasy.

I could tell he had misunderstood from his words and the sympathy in his expression.

"I wasn't abused, despite what you may believe. God, no, that isn't the case at all. And then I muttered too loudly, "the opposite actually," for reasons that are only known to the goddess.

Matt remained silent, but it was clear from his eyes that he didn't understand. We sat for a minute, perhaps two, in silence.

In an attempt to calm myself, I took a look around his studio and wondered if I would be able to work with this man for whom I had intense feelings. A dozen drawings were affixed to the wall, while unframed paintings were placed on the floor, leaning against the identical pair of walls.

Every sketch included only faces or portions of faces. Mouths and eyes.

With the exception of the dead frogs, however, the paintings depicted whole, nude bodies. Two males and four ladies. Everything is flawless. Models fit for a magazine.

Since Matt pulled me back from my thoughts—which were still fixated on his hard-on—I suppose I had been staring at him for too long.

"What are you contemplating?"

To be honest?Your cockier."

"Words cannot express how much I wish that had never occurred."

"Is there a medical issue with it or something?"

"A what? No, not unless you think it's a medical problem to develop a boner when a pretty woman says she wants a quickie. A psychological disorder? That's for certain.

How come? That's not how I—

"I am aware. You didn't mean to say that. Or precisely what you mentioned. Put it down to wishful thinking. And I really apologize. Indeed, I am.

My girl gear brought me some joy, but the thought of the one male who had ever expressed interest in getting naked with me made my heart bleed with shame.

"Any woman could be on this campus." You have ladies pleading with you to undress them, after all.

"And none of them should be seen in their pants. Abbie, why are you unable to comprehend this?

"Maybe we simply let it go? If you don't mind, I don't want to think about nude bodies.

Sadly, ever since I met you, all I can think about is nude bodies—yours specifically. And following this brief instance of... "I don't think I should register for this course, Abbie," he groaned, lowering his head. I'm concerned that I could put you through too much discomfort. I apologize.

IT HURTS TO REPEAT

Even so, congrats if your time together is dominated by passionate encounters and you're still in the early stages of courtship. Take it all in. However, it might be difficult to be present when there are competing demands for your attention, especially when she is with her partner.

She may miss another great opportunity to spend quality time with her partner if she thinks about her work at night or in the morning. Worrying about unspoken mishaps at work is probably the worst enemy of spontaneous kissing.

A common technique in awareness practices that might assist you in moving out of your head and into your body is to counteract the inclination to cognitively focus on what you can see, hear, smell, taste, and feel. A thoughtful kiss with your significant other is similar to this. We both begin breathing in unison, which helps me to relax. All is well in the world. Allow your lips to linger, even for brief kisses.

The intense lip cinch you might want after hours is drastically different from the sweet forepart kiss you want at eight in the morning. However, if all you're planning is a fast kiss as a farewell or greeting, extending the kiss is one of the most overlooked secrets to a wonderful kiss. Actually, it's a sufficiently lengthy kiss.

However, if you take the time to do it, you'll have the chance to truly connect and synchronize with one another, which will make you feel closer.

What takes place when you're syncing?

In terms of chemistry, a great deal, When you kiss, your body releases OxyContin, which makes you feel closer to your partner. Furthermore, research indicates that kissing may increase the feel-good neurotransmitter dopamine while decreasing the stress hormone cortisol. You might experience some ecstasy.

I try to trap her and base her with a longer kiss when she goes into a mode of trying to get a lot done.

Even so, if everyone is comfortable with jargon, introduce it slowly. Some individuals find French kissing, or kissing with language, to be really fun. However, you should always introduce your lingo slowly and sensually into your partner's lips unless you've both decided to go into more violent lingo activity straight away. An unexpected tongue zipping in and out of your lips can be an unpleasant surprise, as you may have experienced.

No matter how many times you've smelled someone's lips, taking your time when it comes to language can not only help you figure out what works with a new partner, but it can also strengthen the bond and make you feel more satisfied.

Magic happens for the mate who gets it right.

Institution, with only a tiny dash of jargon and a sympathetic, compassionate, passionate critique. It's similar to taking a chance on a long-lost, latent sense of who you are.

Likewise, lose themselves in a passionate kiss with the proper person. If there is a connection, though, it feels as though everything stops and you are alone. Take the other person's lead (as long as it feels correct to you) to give yourself the highest odds of reaching just the proper quantum of jargon. Take note of how far they're sticking their tongue in your mouth and equal it. You may also try a little more and observe how they react before moving on to become an even more involved slaver.

It's fashionable to approach slowly and make sure your partner is having fun. For others, engaging in each other's slaver can feel almost intimate.

Melissa believes that less jargon is preferable.

Avoid using overly formal language, as it can become sloppy and overly friendly. Everybody will be talking about that sweet spot.

"Slobber," "sloppy," and "happy slaver medium" are, of course, relative expressions. Is this acceptable? or "Are you fond of that?" Slobber might be someone else's passionate, sensual kissing session. Unless you inquire, you automatically know how your partner who you kiss thinks about a slave. Yes, even something as basic as "Do you like that?" or "Is this okay?"

If you're going to fail, then be kind to yourself.

When a kiss becomes intense, it might turn violent. Some people find that intensity to be light-scented. However,

Pay attention to your partner and experiment with light biting—just not too much. Conquer his lips with ease, then softly suck and tug on them. Erin agrees with a mocking grin and turns her lips.

Chuck's phone rang two hours before their first date. Bonnie was there. Hey, I was about to give you a call. Chuck heard a metallic crash through the phone, then several shouts and what sounded like the screeching of chair legs. "Is everything okay?"

Over the sound of what sounded like a saucepan lid clattering, Bonnie said, "I won't be able to meet you at the restaurant." "My babysitter called in sick, Mara is unavailable as a backup, and the world is ending, as you are surely aware. Grace is freaking out on top of the table because Bethie discovered a mouse in the kitchen cupboard.

After another scream, Bonnie warned someone to be careful around the light fixture. "What brought you to call me?"

The same item. Due to rain delays, my sister is stranded in Oklahoma. Thus, I still possess the guys. Another metallic crash caught his attention. "Are you attempting to use a pot to catch the mouse?"

"No," she chuckled. "I failed to locate any of the traps. Justin believes he can frighten it into the open, where Bethie is ready to sweep it out the door with a broom. Chuck's heart pounded even more when he heard her chuckle. "I had been so excited to see you tonight." He heard her sigh as the background turmoil subsided. "Me, too. However, it appears that all we will do is place a pizza order and stay on mouse patrol. "Rain-check?" "I have a superior concept."

Just as Chuck and his two nephews arrived, THE PIZZAS and sodas were brought. With a bag of mouse traps in hand, Thomas and Nathan hopped out of the vehicle and quickly became friends with Justin, bonding over the idea of placing the sticky square booby traps throughout the kitchen.

When Bethie and Grace heard about the impending battle, they promptly inquired about the critter's well-being after it became lodged.

Grace gulped. "No, mum!"

With surprise, Justin glanced at his sister. "It was you who approached the table, yelling uncontrollably."

"I don't want him dead, even though I find him repulsive."

Grace buried her face as she raced to be by Bonnie's side. Bonnie encircled her daughter's little shoulders with her arms. The way they shook crushed her heart.

A chuckle came from one of Chuck's nephews, but Chuck cut the joke short with a sharp glance.

He knelt down next to them. Hello, Grace. What happens if we capture the mouse and let it outside? Is that acceptable?

Grace gave him a quick glimpse. "You'll not harm him?"

"Assure."

Chuck gave the girls a plastic bottle and instructed them to rinse it out after they had finished eating the pizza and drink. Next, he inquired of Justin whether the garage contained any leftover wood. To find the wire hanger he was looking for, Bonnie hurried to the closet. The layout was cleverly done. Like a see-saw, the bottle balanced on the wire. Chuck put a slice of bread dripping with peanut butter on the floor behind the stove and dropped it into the bottle.

The bottle tips after the mouse gets inside, and he won't be able to get out until we let him.

"Nice." To test the design, the boys tipped the bottle.

"It's awesome." In agreement, Bethie linked her fingers with her twins'. In addition, while he waits, he eats a peanut butter sandwich. That won't bother him at all. Correct, Grace?

Grace nodded while continuing to observe Chuck through doubtful eyes.

The boys had selected an espionage film, and Bonnie said, "And they're out," as the closing titles rolled.

Her two girls were curled up deep in the recliner, while the three boys were spread out across the living room floor in sleeping bags.

"Thanks for letting me bring the boys over," Chuck muttered.

The way the light played with the dark angles of his body and face warmed her to her toes, and his smile raised her heart rate to incredible heights. Bonnie's thoughts raced, trying to think of something safe to talk about. "Justin was overjoyed. It was the first time he had not felt overpowered by numbers. Bonnie moved to face him on her end of the couch. "I apologize for having to cancel on you tonight."

He pivoted. "Why? This is quite pleasant.

Yes? Do you have a penchant for averting disaster in order to save the day?

His eyes flickered, but only briefly. "I was acting with ill intent."

"Guess what, free pizza?"

He didn't think twice. "To give you another kiss."

She cast a peek around the room. "With this crew around, fat chance."

"Come on over here so we can investigate."

It was alluring. With his mischievous lights flickering in his eyes and his cheerful drawl, he was very alluring. Eyes that said it would be enjoyable to kiss him. With him, everything would be enjoyable. If Bonnie allowed him, he would be difficult to resist.

"Chuck—"

There was a single thump in the kitchen as the Coke bottle struck the wood. Like two excited kids, they leaped off the couch and ran to the kitchen to see what they had caught. Chuck raised the trap, taking care not to tip it over. A brownfield mouse twitched its nose in return.

"It appears that the mouse-watch is over," Chuck said.

"I'm happy. It pained me to say it, but I couldn't bear the thought of a mouse running about in here. As the mouse searched for a way out, Bonnie shuddered. He's a little adorable. Grace will be overjoyed that he is safe.

Before Chuck released the mouse into the field beyond the fence, they snapped a photo of him as evidence.

He turned back to wash his hands, finding Bonnie had just completed loading the dishwasher. It seemed natural to stand shoulder-to-shoulder with him. It had been simple going with him tonight. His company had such a basic comforting quality that it enveloped her.

She allowed him to kiss her as he turned to face her and lifted her chin. No, I was way too docile.

Bonnie wants another kiss from him. She was eager to experience warmth, desire, and life again. Desiring him, she put her arms around his waist and drew him in, savoring the way his lips slid over hers as though he was as much enjoying her as she was him. Her lips met his.

When they were out of breath, he pressed his forehead to hers. His hands were around her face. "I've been thinking about that since you brought it up in the coffee shop."

She was rendered dumb by the way he shaped her body to fit his while biting her bottom lip. She attempted to concentrate on his words. "What—what did I say?"

"Coming out."

having sex. Bonnie smiled, barely remembering to utter the words, but she was so happy he did. Ever

since the coffee shop, he had been thinking about her. "Did I say that?"
"You did, indeed." His arms grew closer to her as that cunning sparkle appeared in his eyes. "Want to continue doing it?"
Reaching for him, she pulled him towards her. "Yes, indeed."

Impending Doom

My eyes have teared up, and I have to wait a moment before reading on. A sense of impending doom hangs over the last two letters, but I know I will read them. I have to know how this ends. The second last letter is postmarked 19 February 1945

My Darling Rose,

Your letter was unexpected, and of course, I think it is fantastic news. We are to be a family. I must write and tell my parents.

I was sad to hear your father's being so strict. We will be married as soon as we are able, so he has no reason to accuse you of dishonoring him.

I'm sending some money with our usual courier to make sure you have enough to get some lodgings of your own. It is nice of Carrie to let you stay with her, but her place is small, and you need your own space.

I'm counting the hours until I see you again. I'll try and call you when the phones are back on. Write me and let me know how you are.

All my Love, Marlon

Without taking a breath, I opened the envelope dated 15 May 1945.

My darling Rose,

I've enclosed a copy of the photo James took at the V-Day Celebrations. As you requested, you cannot see your condition. This is one for us to keep and show our children; the other I have close to my chest as it captures our whole family.

It is hard to believe the war is over, in Europe at least. There is an air of hope here, and in that spirit, I have again applied for permission for us to get married. I should hear we can go ahead any day now.

Hold tight, my Love,

Your Marlon.

Oh my freaking god. Grammy got pregnant to a man she never married. What happened after that? I scrabble through the papers at the bottom of the box. There are no more letters. What the hell?

'Grammy, how could you be so cruel? You've left this heartbreaking story, and it hasn't got an ending.'

I push myself up from the floor, stretch, then head to the kitchen. I grab a glass and fill it with water from the tap. Leaning against the bench, I sip the liquid as my mind whirrs.

Grammy wouldn't have left everything so orderly as if in a

timeline for nothing. The answer must be in that box.

Finishing my water, I rinse the glass and leave it on the draining board before heading back to the bedroom, determined to find answers. I take my seat on the floor and pick up the first piece of paper in the box. It's folded in half and is similar to photos I've seen of old telegrams. Telegrams in war have a whole new meaning; my stomach churns.

'No, Grammy, this can't be what I think it is. Please tell me your story doesn't end with this telegram telling you he's dead. What then? Did you miscarry the baby?'

I can almost hear Grammy saying, "goodness Celia, don't be so melodramatic." My lips curl into a smile at the memory of her no-nonsense tone.

Slowly, I opened the fragile paper, careful not to tear it. It is indeed a telegram, but not the one I was thinking it was. The date of transmission at the top is 01 June 1945.

ROSE HAVE ORDERS TO SHIP OUT. WILL CALL WHEN I CAN. STAY SAFE BOTH OF YOU. MONEY COMING VIA COURIER. LOVE YOU.

Did he leave just like that? How could he?

'Celia, lunch.'

I jump guiltily to my feet, telegram still in hand. Glancing around the room, I can see I have achieved very little, and Nana Lila points this out when she enters the room.

'What have you been doing with yourself. You know we only have today to get this done.' Her brows draw together in a frown. 'Seriously, Celia.'

'I'm sorry Nan.' I bend to scoop up the letters. 'I found these, and I got caught up reading them.' Guilt worms around in my stomach. 'I'm sorry I probably shouldn't have.'

I offer the letters to Nan, and she stares at them, making no move to take them.

'What are they?' she finally asks.

I am thrown a little off balance, then. Surely, Grammy hadn't hidden them from everyone. 'You've never seen them before?'

Nan shakes her head. 'No.'

I bend down and pick up the photo. 'They were in a box with this.'

The frown between her brows deepens. 'That's mum... kissing someone who isn't dad.'

'I know, right. So, I just had to read the letters to find out what was going on. You wouldn't believe what Grammy got up to.' The words tumble out.

Finally, Nan takes the letters. 'Come, let's eat lunch and I'll have a look through these.'

Nana Lily reads the letters while we eat the sandwiches and potato chips she bought for lunch. While she finished the last couple, I made a pot of tea and brought the pot and mugs back into the living room. It all looked so sparse, with the paintings and ornaments packed away.

Sitting down, I pour two mugs of Earl Grey and hand one to Nan. She picks it up and then studies the telegram.

'And that's all there is?'

'No, there's more in the box.' I rise to my feet and rush back to the bedroom.

I'm so intent on retrieving the last of the story that I catch my heel on the carpet, stumble forward, and kick the box. The last few items spill across the floor. Grammy's chronological pile is gone, and I'm left with three white envelopes. I've no idea which one we should open next.

The Past and the Present Meet
I take the letters to my chest and head back to the lounge.
"What is the issue?" Nan asks when I walk in.
I acknowledge, "I mixed them up and I have no idea which one is next."
She gives a smile. "Look inside the envelopes and choose one."
When I opened the first one, it appeared to have some official

paperwork inside. Two envelopes are held in the next, one of which is obviously a different letter from Marlon. This needs to come first. I recline in my chair, sip my tea, and then take out Marlon's letter.

"August 15, 1945 is franked," I declare as I open it.

"Oh, that's Victory Day, when World War Two really ended."

My surprised eyes enlarge.

"You forget that the Cold War was still raging and the world was still recovering from the effects of World War II when I was a child."

Of course. Should I read it aloud to you?

Yes, indeed.

I take a seat and begin to read. How I wish I could hold you in my arms, my sweetheart Rose. Our quick conversations are almost sufficient to sustain me, yet they are also insufficient because I am unable to hold you. Knowing that you have been receiving the money I deposited to you gives me peace of mind. You can't work anymore, so it's even more crucial that I take care of you and our child. Although you advised against it, I have transferred my money to a London account, so in the event that I pass away, it is yours. Before you get mad at me, listen to me. I just have to worry about keeping you and the child safe because things aren't great here. So please, don't be too upset and let me finish this. I've been busy these past several weeks, and although I can't tell you much about what I'm doing, I believe I can state that I've successfully applied my mechanical talents to wheeled vehicles. My friend informed me that I was not in the vicinity of the bombing site. Like you, I assume, we are always hearing about new developments in Japan. I'm relieved that I'm not experiencing the trauma. Positively, there are whispers that this will all end shortly. I hope it's so I can return to you in time to meet our little light in the shadows, our baby. "I have to leave now since they are picking up the mail." Be certain that you will always be in my heart, and I am counting down the hours till I can see you again. Marlon, you have always had my love and heart.

During the final lines, my voice faltered. It's very sad, Nana, I say. He loved her so much, even though we know they were never married. Are you certain you had no prior knowledge of this?

Nan gives a headshake. "Mum never mentioned it."

"And since that was the last letter, we'll never know what happened."
"Are you certain?" That third envelope—what's inside?
I lift the flap, peering inside. There are several letters that are addressed to your mother, but the postmarks are from America, and the handwriting is different. They're not the next in line, in my opinion.
I get the other item from the envelope containing Marlon's previous letter. I frown as I turn it over.
"Nan, your name is on it."
I reluctantly extend my hand to meet hers when she reaches out. I removed the official documentation from the mail while she opened and examined it.
I unfold the tri-folded sheaf of papers and smooth them out with

my palm before scanning them. A birth certificate is the first. What I'm reading is almost unbelievable. I flip through the other documents until I come to the last page. This second birth certificate is a little different from the first one; it was produced in Australia.

My mouth falls open. I look up, watching Nan as she wraps off her reading. Her face is streaming with tears. She hands me the pages with trembling hands. After we switched places, I dived right into reading the letter that brought her to tears.

My English flower, my darling Lily.

I have been a coward if you are reading this. For good cause, I have withheld information from you, but you will undoubtedly believe that I ought to have told you before I passed away.

It is my hope that after reading these papers in chronological order, you will be better able to comprehend them. You've read the letters your father, my first Love, wrote to me.

I'm sure you're curious about what transpired when the letters ceased. The day following his final letter, Marlon was slain in Asia. He never witnessed V-Day, so imagine the irony that it was franked on that day. He was killed almost instantaneously when a jeep tire blew out, and the vehicle collided with him. It was an idiotic accident.

One of his army mates, the mate who had been bringing his letters and money, told me about it. He went looking for me at home, telling me what had happened and providing me with the documents that would allow me to access Marlon's savings.

He spent as much time as he could with me since I was inconsolable. Then checked in with me every few days to make sure everything was okay. We spoke about Marlon at first, as we were both really missing him. After the war, he and Marlon planned to become engineers and launch their own business.

It was fitting that he was present when I gave birth to you because he was my connection to Marlon. He was there when I arrived home and when I came to the conclusion that I had to leave London. One day, he showed up with a proposal, and I accepted it.

I consider myself fortunate to have found two wonderful men in my life. One was a slow burn founded on friendship, and the other was an overwhelming love of first loves. My feelings for James were just as intense as my feelings for Marlon.

You were adopted by James when we got to Australia. He was your father, and he always will be. Not only is it evident from the documents we have, but he loved you just as much as he loved your brother Clarence.

James was never allowed to go back to America since he was not entirely demobbed when we left England. You are aware of this. There, you have a second family that you are unaware of. I used to send Marlon's parents letters and pictures of you every few years. Every now and again, they would respond.

They asked me to bring you home to them because they were grieving for their son. Although I couldn't harm James, there is enough information in the letters I kept for you in the previous envelope to locate them if you so choose.

I am aware that you have inquiries. I'm sorry you found out this way, but I'm also sorry I won't be around to respond to them. I loved both of your fathers, which is why I took this route. Out of respect for one, I kept this information to myself and did not share it with you; out of respect for the other, I let you discover it for yourself.

My Lily, I am so proud of the woman you have become. You were everything to your fathers. You can now use this as your legacy in any way you see fit.

Mother, I will always be there for you and adore you.

"Nan, how on earth are you going to handle this?" Glancing up from the now-stained letter with tears, I say.

With tears still trickling down her cheeks, Nana Lily is gazing off into the horizon. It doesn't seem like she heard me.

I take the last envelope's letters out. All of them are native to Brooklyn, New York. "Nan, would you want to read these?" I ask, looking up.

Her eyes eventually come to concentrate on me after a few blinks. "Not right now, Celia, my love."

She wipes her palm across her face, stooping to put the letters back in the box. I stack the Brooklyn letters on top. Though this box belongs to Lily, and it's up to her to determine how much more she reveals, I really want to read them.

"Come on, Celia, let's get to work."

"However," I begin to object, but I change my mind when I notice Nana Lily's dejection.

I go up and give Nan a bear embrace. A few moments later, her tears are all over my T-shirt. I ask, "Nan, would you like me to take you to Mum?" once she stops crying. I may return and do this here.

I walk her to the hall table so she may get my car keys after I feel her nod against my shoulder. She stops me as I open the door and says, "Hold on a minute."

Returning to the table, she takes up the box that holds her

Chapter 3: Getting Past Your Fear

When two people are attracted to each other, they will probably enjoy a passionate kiss. But since it's your first time and you don't know if your partner will accept or reject such a daring approach, this can be a very nervous overture. This kind of worry could prevent you from taking the necessary action to enable your developing romance to fully develop into something truly unique that is worthwhile to preserve or pursue. To get over this fear and start feeling confident about what you are about to do, there are a few things you need to know.

Give Up Criticising Yourself

You may be too hard on yourself or fixated on all the reasons he/she might not like you or want to kiss you, which is one of the reasons you're terrified. Close it down. It's normal if you feel nervous for a little, but that shouldn't stop you from planting the ideal kiss. Give up believing that you lack competence or that you have no idea what you are doing. Worrying about all of these things will just make you more tense and can even ruin that ideal moment. Remind yourself of all the wonderful things about you that make you a desirable catch, and tell yourself you are ready. This will give you more confidence.

Discover How to Do It

Each person gives a somewhat distinct kiss to the next. Once you have perfected the French kissing technique, you will actually have your own method. But because this is your first time, make an effort to understand the fundamentals. Although it will take some time to master the technique, you will know roughly how to execute it.

Get Ready

I gave you some advice on how to get ready for the ideal kiss. Adhere to these instructions, and review the information again to ensure you have not overlooked anything. Being ready and feeling ready will ease your mind, give you peace of mind, and give you more self-assurance. Prepare the location, choose, clean, and hang your attire properly, and have chapstick and mints ready.

Although everyone can French kiss, mastering the fundamentals or the art of the kiss will require some basic technique learning. After gently kissing each other, a French kiss is more than just putting your tongue on their lips. Rather, it's a delightful and sensual tongue action that you can do with your spouse. It's a very private kissing method, and knowing the fundamentals will offer you some much-needed grace.

You should first practice regular kissing before attempting a French kiss. Before you give someone a French kiss, you can wait a few more dates, hours, or even minutes. You can also go on to French kissing in a matter of seconds. You and your lover should move at a pace that suits you both. Because French kissing is so personal, it truly only works when both of you are at ease with one another. French kisses typically occur spontaneously (after the initial "regular" kiss) and don't require any preparation. However, if your spouse is reticent or bashful, you can try talking to them about it or just quietly express your tolerance and readiness to wait. Your partner might become comfortable enough to agree to it only based on that. Alternatively, it's possible that they simply require some motivation, particularly if this is their first time.

Typical Kissing Initially

A normal kiss should come first, and the French kiss will follow organically. Work your way up to the French kiss by beginning with tiny, delicate kisses delivered with relaxed lips. Keep in mind that you should both appreciate and enjoy the sensation of these casual yet intimate kisses before attempting a French kiss. Tickle the Lips

You can gradually go from the gentle kissing phase to the French kissing phase by slowly and lightly dabbing your partner's lips with the tip of your tongue. This is a charming and private approach to indicate to your lover that you are open to new experiences.

Time to Investigate

You can attempt to make tongue contact with your lover after you've both kissed. You can accomplish this by softly kissing your partner's lips with your tongue. When their mouth opens slightly, you will know that he or she is accepting your invitation. After that, you can start your exploration gradually. As you explore, be sure to vary the duration of your tongue contact. Your partner will express their comfort level and level of interest in what you are doing through their body language. If this doesn't feel natural to you and your companion, it will simply sour the experience.

This is a tip for using your tongue to explore your partner's mouth. It should be slightly pointed but not overly taut or muscular. Make sure it's not very soft, like a dead clam.

You should have that in-between tongue position. Like you're licking off a tiny glob of ketchup that you just spilled on your wrist. That's roughly the force and pressure of your tongue that you want.

You might begin gently swirling around your partner's tongue after moving your tongue to make different durations of contact with it. When executed correctly, this is one of the most alluring aspects of French kissing. You can accomplish this by gently rubbing the tips of your tongue against those of your partner, allowing a small amount of overlap. It's important to ensure that this is done sensually and intimately, so proceed with caution and gentleness. Since this is your first time, you shouldn't be kissing aggressively just now unless your partner initiates it.

Avoid sticking your tongue too long in your partner's mouth. Initially, a few seconds suffice. Reposition your tongue and give your partner's lower lip a quick nibble to stir things up once more. To avoid hurting your spouse and ruining the ideal moment for the two of you, make sure you merely nibble rather than bite. You can get your spouse to lock their lips longer by nibbling their lower lip.

After that, if your partner is confident enough to start it, you might feel your partner inserting their tongue in your mouth in a manner identical to your previous interactions. A little back-and-forth is included, interspersed with frequent, smaller kisses and lip nibbling. The secret is to avoid making things uncomfortable or awkward by not standing still for an extended period of time.

Other Audacious Steps

Sucking, or applying a tiny bit of suction, is an excellent technique to use during French kissing. This gives your French kiss a new twist, but it's a brave and dangerous move to do, particularly if you're a beginner. It's important to keep in mind that you can only do this if your spouse has consented to the French kiss. When your significant other uses their tongue to probe your mouth, softly seize it, suck on it for a brief moment, and then let go. You can anticipate that your spouse would stick their tongue out for more if they enjoy it. You might also feel some suction the next time your tongue touches his or her mouth after you've taught them this new technique. Here, it's important to be gentle. Super-suctioning is quite unpleasant and will make you appear extremely inexperienced.

Another risky move you may take during a French kiss is to stick out your tongue all the way, as this can elicit a very passionate response from your partner. You shouldn't go overboard, though, as this could make your partner gag, which would spoil any chance of a beautiful or otherwise intense kiss. If you're not sure, don't stick your tongue out too far.

Increased Physical Touch

There is intimate physical contact during a French kiss. When you are apart from your partner, this is something you can never do. For as long as the kiss lasts and even after it's ended, you should remain hugging and holding each other.

Even if you're encircling each other with your arms, you can improve the kiss even further by softly stroking, rubbing, or squeezing each other in the background. During this type of close kiss, your tongue and lips may move in different directions. Additionally, there can come a moment when your lips will relax and gently trace onto the person's cheeks, earlobe, chin, and neck. However, you need to be aware of how your spouse appears to be comfortable and understanding with this. This is a positive indication of approval if they turn their head back or tilt the portion of their body you're kissing closer to you so you can get at it more easily. This is going to be quite personal, and your body will probably feel energized. Since this is the first time, you also need to be ready to recognize your own and your partner's boundaries; you need to know when to stop.

Even in highly emotional and intimate moments, you should never go beyond what seems proper. Refrain from touching areas of their body that might be too soon to examine with your hands. You can very well anticipate that if your first kiss goes well, you'll have lots of opportunities to kiss later on and spare time for other activities. You should keep your hands in places that aren't overly invasive unless your date makes it very obvious that they like what you're doing and where you're putting them.

Maintain a Busy but Orderly Hands

Now that your mouth is occupied, what do you do with your hands? Do you let them walk around freely? Don't do that unless your goal is to make your date freak out or run away. Additionally, avoid simply standing there with your hands in your pockets or hanging there. This is what you ought to do: Initially, place your hands on your partner's back or sides. You might slide your hand down your partner's neck, run it through their hair (this works better on girls), or gently cup their cheeks to intensify the intensity.

You could move your hands along your partner's sides to get more daring if you're the adventurous kind. Keep them a few inches apart instead of moving them to key spots; after all, this is your first kiss, and you don't want to come across as hurried.

Don't Say Much on Your Tongue

Avoid sticking your tongue out and kissing your spouse on the first kiss. Don't, however, conceal it either. Simply touch your date's lips with the tip of your tongue. If the person you are dating feels comfortable with you, you are doing something right. You can now be brave and delve a little deeper (with your tongue).

How long is ideal for a first kiss to last?

It's crucial that first-time kissers ask themselves this question. In order to avoid being too lengthy or too short, how long should the first kiss last? How long does the ideal first kiss last?

The passionate moment's meter is used to measure first kisses instead of seconds. You shouldn't focus on planting the ideal kiss. Make an effort to kiss someone with passion and timing. For example, give your date a quick kiss and turn your head slightly away from their face. In addition to allowing the feelings to "flow," this allows you to read your date's expression and determine whether the kiss was successful. You can then move on based on the expression.

Don't Press It

Those who kiss for the first time skip this stage. Your date might not always approve of your touching or kissing behavior. Most of the time, we misinterpret resistance as being bashful, playing hard to get, or inviting a challenge. After that, we keep going. What happens if your partner declines to be touched or kissed at that moment?

Give up being aggressive if, after a few tries, you encounter resistance. Keep your chances of getting another date intact, and don't let being pushy destroy yours. Keep your cool; more opportunities for kissing will present themselves.

Adolescent Love, ardor, and caution Love is wonderful, but it's also dangerous. You will have the most amazing and thrilling experiences of your life when you are in Love. But the most agonizing times will also come while you're in Love. It's possible that the person you love the most causes you the most pain.

The sad truth is that you can never compare another person's Love to your own, no matter how much you love them. Because of this, you should cherish the wonderful times you had with your first Love while still exercising caution and being ready for bad things to happen. Let us discuss the ardor and prudence of adolescent Love.

Recognizing The Passion

You will feel a great deal of passion when you first fall in Love because that is what youthful and initial Love is all about.

You find him/her to be very, very cute. You have a purpose to live, or even breathe, thanks to your new Love. You feel unable to be somewhere that your lover isn't, and when you are, you can't wait to see them again. You want to take your partner everywhere with you.

You share your deepest emotions and accomplish everything together. You believe that person to be your soul mate and that there is no one else in the world fit for you. The way you glow at each other when you stare at each other, everyone can tell you two are in Love.

Passion has the power to erase all other thoughts. It will cause you to forget about your schooling, family ties, responsibilities, and homework. It will teach you to put less value on your basketball or football practices since spending time with "the love of your life" is more important than everything else. You'll forget about your pals and stay away from your parents (particularly if they don't approve of the relationship).

It's important to ask yourself, "What will you do when all the passion and excitement melts away?" because, regrettably, that is what will probably happen.

How to Apply Imagination

Make sensible use of your passion. Allow it to inspire you, teach you new things about yourself, and help you comprehend the reason behind your Love for the person you care about. In order to become a person who appeals to both yourself and other people, try to learn how to balance your emotions, confidence, and sense of self-worth.

Furthermore, don't put your obligations, friends, and family on the back burner in favor of your romantic partner. The individuals who will support you when the thrill wanes are your family and friends. You will have wasted time on something that is not as vital as the tasks you neglected if you ignore them.

It is not the end of life; therefore, resist the urge to let youthful passion and love destroy you. Thus, this kind of advice is nonsensical when you're a teenager and in your sweet sixteen (don't be this dumb). Allow your recently discovered

Love to serve as your adult education ground. Keep your eyes on the intense passion and heat of adolescent Love. Rather, let your initial engagement serve as a blueprint for creating wholesome relationships. This puts you in a successful relationship going forward.

Your first Love transports you to a realm of emotions beyond anything you have ever known. It's simple to become disoriented and forget who you are in the heat of the moment. You have a lot ahead of you as you start your life, including achievements and possibly a lot more relationships. This is the reason you must maintain your composure in the face of emotion and excitement. Here's how to carry that out:

How to Approach Your First Date with a Clear Head

It is uncommon, no matter how much Love you feel, that the person you spend the rest of your life with is your first Love. Teens who are in love frequently fantasize about living happily ever after with the first person they fell in love with. It is highly improbable that your first or second Love will end up being your final one. These "dreams" are quite unrealistic. Love is plenty, so don't cling tenaciously to a relationship under the mistaken impression that it's the only one out there for you.

You Are Loved; Have Faith in It

If someone tells you that your Love is small and unimportant, don't believe them. Adults frequently refer to childhood love as "puppy love" and think it's merely a fleeting feeling. However, don't let the fact that it was "puppy love" make you disregard your first romantic encounter.

Enjoy, explore, and find yourself in your first Love, which is perhaps the purest Love you will ever know. But exercise caution and refrain from attempting to demonstrate the validity of your Love by expressing it in the same manner as passionate adult love. Have faith that even in its innocence, your "puppy love" qualifies as Love.

Remember that Love and sex are not the same thing.

You may feel loved after having sex, but you won't feel loved after having sex. It's possible that your lover is only craving for you and is not truly in Love with you if you have sex. You should not abuse sex in your quest for Love. A true love partner won't ask for a "sex bribe" in order to be in your company.

Everything you do from now on, you should be mature and responsible enough to manage any possible fallout, including the possibility of getting pregnant and contracting STDs. You are not allowed to have sex if you find that you are unable to handle these; wait until you are able to handle the repercussions before having sex.

Take Your Time.

You have no need to fit in just because everyone else is dating and falling in love. Go on dates only if you truly want to, when you are confident that you have discovered the one you truly love, and when you are aware of who you are. If not, just remain single and, if necessary, go out with your buddies.

Love Someone Who Returns The Love

Unrequited and selfish loves are not the greatest kinds on which to base a relationship, as previously said. When Love is not reciprocated, it can negatively impact your self-worth and even make you doubt your deservingness of Love. Selfish and unrequited Love can lead to self-doubting thoughts such as "What is wrong with me?" "What went wrong with me?" "Do I dress well, or am I just not attractive enough to be loved?"

Mutual respect and Love are the foundation of a strong relationship. Do not believe that there is a problem with you if the person you love does not reciprocate your feelings. All you haven't done is find "the one."

Before you talk about social media, talk about it first.

Young people, in particular, are powerless to stop it.

But not everyone desires to have their every action publicly shared on social media. For this reason, discuss with each other what aspects of your relationship—or each other—you should post on or avoid on social media. Say so if you do not want him/her to post your pictures.

Protect Yourself Against Influence

You're probably not familiar with a lot of things your spouse would wish to do or things that other people are doing when you fall in Love for the first time. You might succumb to the pressure as a result. For example, the majority of teenagers who had sex during their initial dating days confess that they did so out of need rather than choice.

Protect yourself from the demands placed upon you. Nothing you don't want to do or are ill-prepared for has to be done. Before you do anything, mentally prepare for everything. Make a decision early on and communicate your ideals and your willingness to compromise to both your partner and yourself. This prevents you from acting rashly when things get tight. What makes most of us succumb to pressure is not being prepared.

However, pressure does not equal love; if someone puts you under pressure, it is likely because they do not genuinely love or need you as much as you believe.

It's alright to walk away if necessary.

Since your first love was the only one you had experienced up until that point—aside from your family and friends—it could seem like the only love you will ever know. This is the reason you are probably occasionally hanging on for dear life when things are not going well.

It's acceptable to end a relationship if it's not working, your partner has changed, or you believe you deserve more. We occasionally have a tendency to hang onto unsatisfactory relationships out of fear of upsetting the other person or out of a desire to avoid hurting them.

It will sting to let go of someone you love, but it's a necessary step.

Yes, you will hurt, but only temporarily. After that, you will recover, grin once again, and be free to discover love that is unconditional.

4 Constance

Although she preferred the Americanized form of Constance, the nanny's real name was Constancia. She was reared mostly in the less expensive city of Nuevo Laredo, Mexico, after being born in the US twenty years ago. Even as a small child, she was aware that she wasn't as quick-witted as the other girls while they were playing games like hand slapping or picking up the pebbles, but she was fine with that. Her mind operated more like one of those steady goods trains that pass the border bridge, full of illegal immigrants hoping to hitchhike to the Promised Land.

Fernanda uttered the words "there" as the infant took her final breath and drifted off to sleep. Constance observed while Fernanda covered and carefully placed the child in the cot. With a smile, Fernanda added, "I have some good news for you," to Constance. "I was informed by Randy that you could travel to Paris with us. The infant and you. Should you so desire?

Of course, Constance replied. "I would adore to attend." She briefly held Fernanda's hands while feeling her heart pound behind her ears.

"Do you possess your passport?"

"Yes."

Fernanda said, "I just feel uneasy leaving the baby."

Constance loved Fernanda very much. She was as near to a blood relative as she would ever know despite not being one. In contrast to Randy, Fernanda expressed her appreciation for Constance's fervent devotion to the Catholic Church, finding it both consoling and endearing.

She was filled with inspiration as she walked past the cot. She and Fernanda were visiting the Crown. To make contact with the Crown! Is it possible for you to imagine? The Real Crown. To make contact with it! All of your misdeeds and ailments would undoubtedly go. Poof.

With a smile, Fernanda caressed Constance's head. "For those who have faith," she uttered. "For people who are similar to you."

Constance bolted upstairs to her little room in the cabin's attic, with its exposed ceiling beams and small window looking out over the exposed mine. She looked out and watched the massive quartz veins in the mine sparkle in the morning sun. Then, she sat on her bed and opened the laptop Randy had purchased for her when she first arrived to reside with them. Randy had commented, "That won't do," upon seeing her old, broken-down computer.

Attempting to control her emotions, she signed onto the PEOPLE site and wrote as intelligently as she could in her most recent remark on the still-active discussion about Fernanda, titled Fernanda the Innocent.

"I have verified Fernanda the Innocent's departure for Paris. I've received an invitation to join her and witness what may be the second-biggest gathering in Church history. Maybe this is the time that a lot of us have been looking forward to. Why am I saying this? Consider it! Paris. The location of the Crown of Thorns.The sacred Crown that covered His head during His crucifixion. Consider! She is headed to the city where the Crown of Thorns is located.

She waited for the comments after clicking Send, certain that this post would cause a snowball to fall. It was her favorite way to engage with the outside world. She had never interacted with anyone in that way back on the border, with actual people. She felt free to express her true beliefs on the internet. Every voice was equal, and every anonymous individual on the internet was lovely. Lovely spirits.Making contact.contacting without actually touching. You could do anything on the internet.

5. Ed's Thorn in the side

Situated just outside of Pittsburgh, the Saint Anthony Chapel is a grand white-stone Catholic cathedral featuring twin bell towers topped with gold crosses. It is home to the world's second-largest collection of sacred relics, second only to the Vatican. FBI agent Ed Pushkin felt a streak of white lightning pass across the left side of his chest as he ascended the building's third step. Heart palpitations? After all, he was about sixty years old and comfortably overweight by twenty pounds. But no—just an unexplained ache that vanished as fast as it appeared, leaving behind the recollection of Peru and that dreadful ten thousand-step walk in the Andes that followed the suspect in his previous case, Fernanda the Ripper. The Beautiful

Fernanda. That walk had cost him dearly; he had come dangerously close to death. Asked for a three-month break in order to heal completely. They moved him to his previous role with the FBI after he returned. A desk job first. And lastly, this new case—the Holy Thorn case—the Saint Anthony's burglary. His aged, veined hand gripped the chilly doorknob. He hesitated, wondering what strange things Chance, Fernanda's ex-boyfriend, and her husband Randy were up to. He had to acknowledge that they were missing. Together, that had been an incredible walk. Would he ever find such companionship and adventure again? Maybe the saints, whose fragments were kept in gold boxes within this church, knew something. Would inform him.

These were peculiar times. The tech bubble has burst. The Catholic Church faces insolvency as a result of its cover-up of priests who engage in sexual misconduct. Online groups emerged, where gossip frequently took precedence over the facts. Did these events portend the end of the world? It was his first church attendance since his twenties. I had no idea he would be so moved when he stood at this one's door. Dread and loneliness overcame him. A flash of insight that he will die well before his time.

He pushed the door open. A rumor of long-dead things mixed with the smell of burning candles. He moved forward to the final row of wooden pews in the large church with the wall-mounted Stations of the Cross exhibitions and stained glass windows. There was a great deal of suffering there, with Christ going through unending agony and having no one to assist him. Ed heard the heavy door click firmly shut behind him. Ed experienced a constriction in his chest, as though the church, adorned with Christian symbols and walls covered with relics, was enclosing him, encasing him like a tomb. A shadowy figure came towards him.

The middle-aged man in the white collar and black robe remarked, "Welcome." His delicate features clashed with his crewcut. "Father Matthew of the Saint Anthony parish, I am."

Ed said, "I'm FBI." He scrabbled to find his badge. I'm rusty at this, Rusty thought to himself.

"So, you're here roughly?"

"The pilfered artefact," Ed concluded for him. "An ancient plant, I think?"

"You could refer to it as that," smiled Father Matthew. But in reality, a thorn. From the Thorn Crown. It is among our most treasured treasures. Our wood from the Cross itself comes in second only. He turned, and Ed felt that, in that robe, he moved a little too elegantly, more womanly than manly. "I'd like to give you a tour," he gestured.

Ceramic dioramas of Christ on the Cross, three-quarter size, were distributed by them. Ed never really got the feeling that a man—a god, perhaps?—was being tortured to death. Nevertheless, he believed it to be a fairly accurate metaphor for his own life—the agony of needing to support oneself and the agony of a woman who has Alzheimer's disease gone insane. His ordeal had lasted quite some time. Yes, he had a bad attitude this morning.

Father Matthew stated, "We have over five thousand relics of the first and second class."

Ed questioned, "First and second class?"

"Excellent as components of a saint's body or as tools used during Christ's Passion. Father Matthew clarified, "Second class being something the saints owned or something used to torture them." Ed became irritated as his eyes glistened. "Anything that has come into contact with a first or second-class relic is third-class."

They came to a halt in front of an exhibit featuring gold lockets, each containing a saint's tooth, shard of bone, or hair.

"So I would be a third class relic if I touched one of these?"

"If you choose to consider yourself as such," Father Matthew grinned once again.

Ed stated, "The younger agents at the office already do." He had to smile in return. Father Matthew extended a locket, allowing Ed to come into contact with the ancient bone fragment that was securely enclosed.

Ed questioned, reaching out and tapping the bone with a finger, "Does it have magic power?" "Does touching me grant me access to magic power?"

Father Matthew remarked, "The Bible claims that even the touch of Saint Peter's shadow cured the sick." "Magic ability? Indeed. You could call Faith that, I suppose.

Ed questioned, "Which saint is it from?"

"Saint Jude," remarked the priest. "The patron saint of lost causes."

"Well picked," Ed exclaimed. "So every saint has a particularity?"

Father Matthew responded, "The majority do, and October 28th is his feast day." He removed another locket from the wall and placed the relic of Saint Jude up. "Saint Philomena's hair." She works well with lost causes as well.

Ed also ran a hand over the hair. Felt the hair on the back of his neck stand up. He enquired, "How did she die?"

"Excellently," expressed Father Matthew. One day, Emperor Diocletian spotted her by the baths and decided to make her his new bride. Refusing, she explained to him that she had given her virginity to Jesus. In the hopes that pain would make her change her mind, he had her imprisoned and flogged.

Ed remarked, "I guess back then they didn't know that chocolate and flowers could win a woman over."

Father Matthew stated, "She had disregarded the Emperor." Thus, the torment served as both a form of punishment and persuasion. His tone took on the cadence of a sermon as though he was getting comfortable sharing a tale he had heard many times. Even after receiving severe whippings, Philomena refused to consent to marry the Emperor. Diocletian was then cast into the river with an anchor fastened around her neck. She miraculously surfaced, unencumbered by the anchor. He ordered his men to drill the girl with arrows because he was frustrated that she would not give in and, worse yet, would not perish. Still, not an arrow struck her heart. Breathless, bleeding, and bruised from the whipping, with arrows protruding from her chest, she lifted her head and whispered her unwavering confidence in Jesus Christ. A murmur that sent the Emperor reeling. She perished while remaining faithful to our Lord when he gave his men the order to chop off her head.

Ed exclaimed, "Wow."

The dad gave a nod. "Many miracles have been performed over the centuries with her relics."

Ed thought That's not a pretty way to go out. It's a terrible way to pass away. And it was via that touch that he had touched her hair and received her wild stubbornness. Or much worse.

Ed was tired. That would account for his grumpiness. Continued to wake up yesterday night. His glass eye was scratchy, too.

Father Matthew declared, "We revere these relics because they serve as a reminder of the many holy men and women who gave their lives in the service of Christ, our Saviour."

They went from the locket wall to a glass display case filled with treasures that resembled trophies. A gap in the casing was covered with tape. The case was opened by Father Matthew.

"A slam dunk," Ed exclaimed.

Father Matthew remarked, "A smash, yes, but more of a careful extraction than a grab."

These are our sacred objects. Plated in gold and silver and embellished with semi-precious stones. This one was in possession of the lost Thorn. Originates in 1600.

"Don't touch it," Ed commanded.

Indeed, the authorities have already checked for prints. None of them piqued my curiosity.

But hold on, Ed said. "What is the approximate value of this reliquary and trophy?"

Father Matthew responded, "It is priceless to me."

"How much is it worth to the pawnbroker in downtown Pittsburgh, though?"

The frame is coated in gold. Worth a minimum of one thousand dollars, according to Father Matthew. "It could be worth much more if you found the right buyer—

someone who was more interested in the relic than the gold."

"Interesting," Ed remarked. "Plus, they didn't take it."

Not at all. The Holy Thorn alone.

Ed rubbed the hair from his chin.

"And what's the value of that thorn?" he inquired.

"The Holy Thorn has great value," remarked Father Matthew.

"I get it for you, but?"

"If I had to charge for it," Father Matthew remarked. "I would almost certainly charge a million dollars for the Thorn."

Ed took a second look. I needed to take a moment to process that. A $50 million thorn. Excellent relic. Furthermore, they refused to accept the container, whose gold might have been melted down and sold without running any risks. His curiosity was aroused, and his inner investigator reawakened.

"And how much do you think all of these other reliquaries and relics here are worth?"

Father Matthew apologized, saying, "I don't like to think of all these marvels in terms of money."

Ed asked, "You're attached to all of this, aren't you?" "Intimate bond"

Father Matthew declared, "They are my children." "The artifacts' true value is not measured in US dollars. That error is conceivable but consider it. What is the value of a baby's laugh? How much does a lover's smile cost? Our freedom to worship is precious, but at what cost? If the only consideration for anything is its monetary worth, then not everything can be valued fairly.

Ed answered, "I understand, Father," sounding a little like he was in Sunday school. Alright. So tell me a little about the Thorn's history. Thus, I now have a clearer understanding of why they stole it and fled the container.

Father Matthew inhaled deeply and exhaled gradually. He went on to say that they would have to start at the beginning if Ed was truly interested in learning about the Thorn. Let us begin in the year 300 with the establishment of Constantinople, the new capital of Roman Byzantium under Emperor Constantine.

"No," Ed interrupted him. "It's not my intention for you to go back that far."

But in this instance, I believe it could be useful. To comprehend the significance of the Holy Thorn and the reasons behind its possible theft.

"All right," replied Ed. "Is it possible for us to sit down?"

"Yes, I apologise. Where are my manners?" Father Matthew would have to round past Ed and take a seat in front of his good eye because he occupied the first row and left no room at the end.

Father Matthew went on. As Emperor Constantine established a new capital in modern-day Istanbul, he became embroiled in a power battle with Rome and the Catholic hierarchy situated there, for he desired to remove not only the governmental but also the religious authority from Rome. In order to achieve this, he dispatched his mother, Saint Helena, to Jerusalem in order to gather whatever relics she could and transport them—as well as the power they held—to Constantinople.

Ed gave the man a quick glance before glancing forward and listening as carefully as his mood let.

The most significant artifacts that Saint Helena discovered during her auspicious search were the Crown of Thorns, the Cross, and the Nails.

"Had she discovered the Cross? Three centuries following the crucifixion?

"Yes, three hundred years after the Passion of Christ," Father Matthew responded. "Someone recognized the significance of the occasion and preserved what is known as relics."

"Tributaries," Ed murmured.

"If you'd like. As you mentioned, these Jerusalem-based religious seekers took Saint Helena to the three crosses that had been in their family for many years. Christ's and the two thieves' crucifixion crosses. So, how could she choose which cross to bring back to Constantinople? Do you have any notion, Mr. FBI?

"I have no idea," Ed replied.

She had each Cross touched by a woman who was terminally sick. Nothing happened when the sick woman touched the first one. Nothing at all in the second. However, upon touching the third Cross, she..."

"She recovered."

Ed guessed, and Father Matthew acknowledged it with a nod.

"She was," Father Matthew confirmed. "Right away. Saint Helena knew she had the correct Cross because of this.

"And the Thorn Crown?"

She discovered the intricately woven Crown of Thorns, but she was forbidden from removing it from the Jerusalem cathedral that housed it. She could only take so many Holy Thorns. The actual Crown of Thorns was sent to Constantinople in 1063 for safekeeping after remaining in Jerusalem for seven more centuries. Two centuries later, right before the Byzantine Empire fell, Emperor Baldwin II awarded the French king the Crown of Thorns. He neglected to add, though, that he had given Venetian moneylenders the Crown as collateral.

Ed remarked, "Aw, so relics do get pawned."

"A vile incident," Father Matthew remarked. He rubbed his signet ring while sitting silently. They both looked up at a chirp and a desperate fluttering of wings. A bird was searching for a way out of the church, high in a dimly lit corner. "I'll find him on the floor, exhausted, after a day or two."

Before he was discovered on the floor, Ed was uncomfortable and wanted to get away. But he required a bit more information. "So the pawn ticket was paid for by the King of France?"

"Louis the IX settled the loan and constructed Saint Chapelle, a reliquary in Paris, to hold the Crown. Notre Dame became the new home of the Crown following the French Revolution. Thorns were taken from the Crown over time and handed to kings, who then gave them to their favorite knights, holy persons, and holy locations all across the world. Over the ages, these Thorns were owned by several people. We were fortunate enough to obtain our own one hundred years ago.

"And it's gone now," Ed remarked.

However, you will locate it for us, Father Matthew added. "Now that the saints' magical power is working in your favour."

Ed answered, "Oh yes." A phone rang, and he jumped. Ed detested the notion that his supervisor might contact him at any time or place, even though these FBI-issue phones were the newest technology.

I apologize, Father. He stood up and moved back a few yards.

One another robbery by thorns. And a homicide as well. The Museum of British Art. Ed listened silently as his boss explained that he had to travel to England, more precisely to the Rothschild estate Waddesdon

Manor. Before he boarded that flight, he also had to call INTERPOL, who suspected a connection to Europe or the Middle East. Ed nodded while listening, and he groaned as he placed his phone away after the call ended.
"I'm grateful, Father. It appears that I'm heading abroad to catch your thief.
"My son, may the saints lead you."
Ed strolled past the porcelain display depicting Christ's suffering and crucifixions.
Father Matthew called after him, "Son."
Ed came to a halt and pivoted halfway. "Yes,"
"Your sight. Remain calm. It appears nice. Very understandable.
"I'm grateful," Ed said. "Daddy?"
"Yes."

"The Thorn. If I did discover it, would you be able to identify it?

The Father responded, "Yes, I would," with unexpected certitude. "My prayers will be for you."

Ed let himself out through the chapel door and into the cool air. He wasn't particularly feeling like taking a transatlantic flight. Already felt jet-lagged. Despite everything that had happened, including the agony of those endless Inca steps, he wished he was back in the Andes. Better yet, to be spending his time off from the FBI back in Russia with his buddy Marina, whom he had met while touring Siberia. Anywhere but on a quest to locate a thorn that has vanished. Now, there are two thorns. First-class relics mixed up with hair and bone fragments from innumerable saints who seemingly all met terrible ends. He pondered if he was meant to be an anonymous saint after all. Beaten to death by life's absurdities. Who, though, would honor his bones?

Chapter 6: An Enchanting Vacation

The guy and the woman made the decision to honor their love with a romantic getaway as they developed their relationship. They decided to spend their relaxing afternoons in the sun, romantic meals by candlelight, and leisurely strolls on the beach at a modest seaside inn.

As they were comfortable in their new room, the woman couldn't help but feel happy. She was appreciative of this peaceful and joyful time as it felt like everything was perfect.

They spent the following several days exploring the area, taking in the local cuisine, perusing antique stores, and spending quality time together. As they strolled down the beach and observed the waves crashing against the sand, they held hands. They discussed their aspirations and the future they wished to create together.

He turned to face her one evening as they were enjoying the sun setting over the ocean on the balcony when he remarked, "I have something to ask you."

With a growing sense of suspense, the woman turned to face him. She enquired, "What is it?"

After inhaling deeply, the man reached inside his pocket. "I know we've only been together for a short time," he replied. Yet it seems like I've known you for a lifetime. I love you so much and can't fathom my existence without you. Will you grant me the privilege of being my spouse?"

Tears appeared in the woman's eyes as her heart leaped with happiness. "Yes," she replied, her voice hardly audible over a sigh. "Yes, I will."

They eventually got engaged, their love as radiant as the stars above. They were aware that obstacles lay ahead, but they also believed that with one other by their side, they could conquer all obstacles.

Chapter 7: The Call of the Future

After their romantic holiday, the man and the woman came home to find themselves engulfed in the chaos of wedding preparations. Dreaming about the life they would create together, they poured hours into choosing flowers, sampling pastries, and going through invitations.

Though busy, there was a lot of happiness at that period. As they collaborated to plan their ideal day, the woman sensed that she was growing more and more in love with him every day.

The woman noticed that she was thinking back on her past and how far she had come as the wedding drew near. Although she had always believed it was impossible, she had always dreamed of discovering real love. And yet here she was, going to tie the knot with her ideal husband.

The woman experienced a wave of serenity on the day of the wedding. As long as she was with the man she loved, she was confident that everything would work out.

She could feel her heart pounding quickly in her chest as she made her way down the aisle towards him. She realized they were meant to be together when she looked up and saw the love in his eyes.

They vowed to love and cherish one another forever when they exchanged vows. The woman also experienced a sense of fulfillment as they shared their first kiss as husband and wife, as if everything had finally come together in her life.

The woman turned to face their friends and family, who had all come to celebrate their love, as the reception got underway. She was appreciative of their help and confident that they would stick by one another through whatever came next.

Thus, the man and the woman set off on their new life together, prepared to meet anything that came their way with love and tenacity. Although they were aware that life would not always be simple, they felt that as long as they had each other, they could overcome anything.

Chapter 8: Obstacles and Successes
The man and the woman discovered that married life was not always simple as they got used to it. Although there were arguments and conflicts at times, they were committed to resolving them amicably.

Despite all of the difficulties they encountered, they never lost sight of their love for one another. As they experienced these setbacks and victories together, they discovered that their devotion to one another only got stronger.

When the man lost his work, it was one of their major problems. They were having a hard time making ends meet and deciding what to do next. However, the woman supported and loved him during every stage of the journey, which helped him stay positive.

After a while, the man was able to find employment again, and things started to get better. They once again dreamed about the future and all the things they wanted to do as a couple.

They had adventures, traveling to new areas and attempting novel experiences. They shared tears, laughed together, and matured as a group. They discovered that love involved supporting one another throughout difficult times as well as happy ones.

The man and the lady reflected on everything they had been through and everything they had accomplished as a couple as they celebrated their fifth wedding anniversary. They were eager for all the adventures that awaited them because they knew that their love had only gotten stronger.

They were prepared to face life's obstacles together, with love in their hearts and a resolve to never give up on one another, even though they knew that challenges would always arise.

Thus, the man and the lady led their lives together, with their love serving as a lighthouse in the shadows that pointed them in the direction of their goals.

The guy and the woman realized that a new chapter was about to start as they turned their gaze to the future. They were eager to see what the future held and had discussed forming a family.

They soon learned the much-anticipated news: the wife was expecting a child. Feeling ecstatic, they daydreamed for hours about the characteristics of their child, their appearance, and their family life.

Although the woman faced difficulties during her pregnancy, the man supported her at every turn. Together, they experienced the pleasures and anxieties of pregnancy, and he helped her when she was unwell or exhausted.

The man and the wife got ready for their baby's arrival as the due date drew near. They purchased all the required items, decorated a nursery, and looked forward to the day when they could finally hold their child in their arms.

At last, the day came. The man hurried the woman to the hospital when she went into labor. Their child, a healthy and gorgeous baby boy, was born after a protracted and challenging labor.

The man and the lady were overcome with love and excitement as they held their son in their arms. They were aware of the permanent changes in their lives and their newfound responsibility for this fleeting little life.

The man and the woman adapted to their new life as parents in the days and weeks that followed. They went through endless feedings and restless nights, but they also felt the unadulterated happiness that comes from seeing their child grow and change.

Gazing into their son's eyes, they perceived a promising and limitless future in front of them. They were aware that they had been given a gift, and they were determined to give their child the greatest upbringing possible.

Thus, a new chapter full of love, happiness, and limitless prospects for the future was written in the lives of the man and the lady.

www.ingramcontent.com/pod-product-compliance
Lightning Source LLC
Chambersburg PA
CBHW052141110526
44591CB00012B/1807